So I Wrote You A Poem

So I Wrote You A Poem

David Tensen

*poems of empathy
on life, loss and faith*

ST MACRINA PRESS

Copyright © 2021 by David Tensen

All rights reserved. No part of this publication may be reproduced, distributed or transmitted in any form or by any means, without prior written permission of the author.

The moral rights of the author have been asserted.

Author website: www.davidtensen.com
Author email: david@davidtensen.com

St. Macrina Press
Abbotsford, BC, Canada

Cover Illustration: Copyright © 2021 David Tensen

Edited: Felicia Murrell
www.yzcounsel.com

Also available in eBook and Audiobook format.

So I Wrote You A Poem / David Tensen. -- 1st ed.
ISBN 978-0-6489893-4-9

Dedicated to those

who find themselves

in midst of these poems.

You are not alone.

Table of Contents

Introduction	1
On Motherhood	9
Poem for Natalie (my wife)	12
For the mother with the autistic girl	10
For the one who terminated a pregnancy and feels ostracised by churches	14
For the tired foster mother of two	17
For the one with postpartum depression	18
For the one unable to bear a child	20
For the mother who worked in emergency services	21
On Trauma	25
For the pastor who nearly died by suicide	28
To the one who…watched their father die slowly	30
'Dear ACOA' For the one with the alcoholic parent	32
For the one recovering from fatigue	35
'Palettes Beyond Pain' For the artist on the healing journey	36
On Religious Shame	39
For the one who comes to church in a wheelchair	44
For the one whose confession set her free	46
For the one who was taken advantage of	48
Poem for the brave	49

On Marriage	51
For the woman waiting for a man to marry	52
For the divorced ones	55
For the one who was betrayed	57
On Everything Else	61
'How to Settle Down' For the wandering migrant	62
How to have hot conversations on conspiracy topics with those you love	63
Enough Words	65
The saving I need	66
About Now	70
A blessing of surrounding	73

Introduction

I'll begin with a confession: Most of these poems were written within one month. Three weeks to be exact. You see, I put a call out on Instagram for followers to send me any stories they would like to put into poetry. I wasn't sure what to expect. Within days, my inbox filled with heart-wrenching narratives on topics like clergy suicide attempts, messy divorces, foster parenting autistic children, abortion, infertility, infidelity, PTSD, partner longings, chronic fatigue, and ostracization in churches for being in a wheelchair or gay. Some poems weren't published and went directly to the requesters. Everything else you read in this book went public on Instagram at the time.

What did 21 days of writing poems for others teach me? Three things:

No one is immune to loss.

Every day that passes is a day gone. Those days may contain life-giving or traumatic experiences. Author Kate Bowler suggests that life is a chronic condition. In many ways, I think it is. Jesus's words, 'In this world, you will have trouble…but take heart, I have overcome!', reminds us we all live on the developing edge of loss and possibility. I believe slowly befriending uncertainty and learning to live with loss, pain and suffering can assist our capacity to love others and self. If we cannot integrate these things into our worldview or personal theology, we will find unhealthy ways to cope.

Poetry gives people permission to feel seen.

Poetry is a profound purveyor of pain. It is the leading language of lament. It is a great holder of hope. A divine gift of healing to the heart. The more poetry I write and read, the more I see the place it has in the world. I am not surprised more than a quarter of the canonised Christian scriptures are, in fact, poetry. More than prose or information, poetry has an ability to make people feel seen, which I think is underrated as a desire intrinsically hardwired into our created beings. Dr. Curt Thompson suggests we're all brought into the world looking for someone that is looking for us, and we never stop searching. I feel that poetry can be to adults what lullabies are to children, a comforting presence (even when the bough breaks and the cradle falls).

Solutions are in abundance today, but poetry seldom offers solutions. Certainty is sold from pulpits most Sundays. But what do you say of a God who meets you in the darkest hour of despair? Answer: You echo Hagar's words in Genesis 16, 'I have now seen the One who sees me.'

I believe being seen is a precursor to reconciliation, and therefore healing. Poetry has the power to heal.

The world desperately needs highly sensitive and empathetic men.

Perhaps now more than ever, with such large-scale loss reminding us of how fragile we all are, we need the emotionally integrated, conscientious and sensitive men of the world to step up. Several years ago, I interviewed Dr. Ted Zeff, a world leading psychologist on raising Highly Sensitive Boys. He noted how different cultures treat boys and men with these traits. In some cases, they are esteemed (e.g., parts of Asia), while in other areas (e.g., the West) they are seen as weak or soft. Yet, fifteen to twenty percent of men have a nervous system that is wired this sensitive way.

As I mention in my last book, *The Wrestle*, I am a Highly Sensitive Person (HSP) and highly empathetic. It is why I've been able to enter into people's stories through poetry, letting them know they are seen and not alone.

I agree with Dr. Elaine Aron; Highly Sensitive People must be given greater recognition in the West as the Priestly Advisors they are, whispering their wisdom of gentleness and care to the zealous and battle-weary Warrior Kings of the world... so we can all survive to live another day.

I have divided this collection into a few themes; however, you will see some poems bleed into others. Two overarching themes kept occurring. Firstly, challenges in parenting - motherhood, in particular. Secondly, a lot poems held layers of frustration, pain and trauma within the context of being a Christian and, in most cases, trying to hold the tension of belonging to a local church whilst feeling ostracised, misrepresented and misunderstood. You will also find poems on marriage, trauma and a few personal pieces towards the end.

I am incredibly grateful for all those who shared their story and helped with the creation of this special collection including Tineke, Ryan and my family. Although a few poems were written with a single story in mind, they are all collectives of other stories I heard during the years I counselled and supported others, particularly Christians, in times of crisis.

As always, you are also free to write me at david@davidtensen.com and share what these poems have meant to you. I do plan to write another volume of these poems for others someday. If you'd like to send me your story, the best thing to do is visit www.davidtensen.com and subscribe to my newsletter so I can let you know about future submission rounds. I am also available for commission-based poetry work. You can easily do this by scanning the QR Code below with your smartphone. It will lead you to the website and any additional resources connected to this book.

With love,

David

SCAN WITH SMARTPHONE FOR URL
AND RELATED RESOURCES

On Motherhood

Natalie and I were married in 1998. We had our first child, a beautiful daughter, after a miscarriage in 2004. Her birth was very traumatic for Natalie and our girl. Our two boys were born a few years later, causing more internal damage for Natalie. The accumulation of birth traumas took its toll, and Natalie developed mental health injuries like post-natal depression and general anxiety disorder. Because of the stigma attached to mental health and the lie we believed, that Christians shouldn't suffer with these kinds of things, most of the injuries, physical and mental were masked and kept in secret. After all, pelvic floor issues and depression are not necessarily visible.

In 2017, we discovered the extent of the damage the traumatic births caused. Pelvic floor muscles had torn away and were irreparable. Urinary incontinence had stolen Natalie's confidence in the workplace and made simple physical tasks difficult and fraught with shame. Major surgery in 2019, and a hysterectomy corrected a huge number of the bladder and bowel problems. We are grateful for the healthcare and expertise available in our area. It made it possible for Natalie to return to work and attend everyday events with far less fear and anxiety.

Natalie's not a perfect mother or wife. And she'll tell you that with a smile. But she is more than enough for my children and me. For over a decade, she endured a whole lot of shame and embarrassment on top of the injuries. She is an incredibly strong and brave soul.

I share these personal things because often our injuries are invisible. Without safe spaces, spouses and communities, too many people, suffer and often over-suffer, especially mothers. The first poem in this section is dedicated to Natalie.

Poem for Natalie (my wife)

Because she refuses
To mortgage her soul
For grandiose masks
That cover the imperfections
She's made peace with

Because she is fierce
When it comes to love
And hate of things
Others avoid touching
Let alone embrace with intention

Because she laughs
No, cackles now
Like her mum does
At things on the edge of naughty
Where joy surprises her with flowers

Because she said yes
To my hand in marriage
And continues to hold it
Refusing to let me fall any way
But in love
With her stubborn daily reply
Yes, and yes again

For the mother with the autistic girl

and it eventually made sense
of all the ways her girl grew different,
that this full-of-life child was awarded
with the esteemed title.

'autism' is neither reward
or punishment for parenting
even though she wrestles with those
questions, still.
autism simply is.

be sure of this,
most parents raising
these gifts are the bravest
of souls, laying down hopes,
dreams, schedules, careers, sleep
and so much more the world takes
for granted.

For the one who terminated a pregnancy and feels ostracised by churches

Oh, how to write a poem
or mention this
particularly in a chapel
without bracing yourself -
as it is the most delicate
and personal of topics
where most involved
are rarely given an audience,
grace or sympathy
for their plight -
regardless of the regret
or shame they carry
for years.

And this is delicate, I know,
for women of faith, or otherwise
to terminate a pregnancy -
marking them as modern-day murderers,
outcasts and heartless
political pawns
without pardon or plea
which are the strangest of sentences
from those quick to forget
that 'thou shalt not murder'
was etched in a stone
held by a man
who ended the life of another
hiding him in the silent sand -
ranking this man of God on mass
among kings, saints and prophets
who did the very same.

And this is delicate, I know
but the silence-endured-partiality of it all
gathers grief
prolongs trauma
heals nothing
and hides behind the lie
that Jesus wept
but she didn't
and grace is insufficient for her
but ample for those
with stones in their hands.

And this is delicate, I know,
because casting stones is easier
than supporting single mothers
or opening homes to foster children
or opening hearts to foster compassion
for those who live with shame
they long to let go of too.

For the tired foster mother of two

and I'm thinking of the single mum
with two foster kids
driving home
from the mental health facility
after one attempted
to give their breath
back to God

and I'm thinking of the security
she must have
to question God
through tired eyes only to hear no answer
but be strengthened enough
to face the uncertain hours ahead.

For the one with postpartum depression

Oh, the expectation!
God knows what we wouldn't give
to spend our lives
two, plus one.

And I waited so long.
And then they came.
 Two lines on a test.
And then she came.
 A baby girl.
And then it came.
 Postpartum depression
  like a debt collector
  for my dreams.
Opposing all the joy
and hopes I had
of being the happy mother
my girl needed
 others needed
  and I needed
   of me.

And I know God is with me.
And for that reason
I won't lie:
These are not the best days of my life,
like the oldies at church say.
They are difficult
Dare I say, terrible at times -
as my whole being adjusts
to what is, for now,
twice as hard as I imagined.

And some days
the bright and shiny me
I dreamt of
makes a guest appearance
but her smile seems staged,
prescribed and pretend
like she's holding to an ideal
and not a growing child
she broke open for
endured for
and loves as fiercely
as I do now.

For the one unable to bear a child

Baby names. One of each. Unused
Prayer. Lots of it. Unanswered
Heart. Aches most days. Unsure
Spare room. Perfect for a child. Unfurnished
Spouse. Leaks from eyes often. Understanding
IVF. Researched and quoted. Unaffordable
Parents. Waiting to be Grand. Unfulfilled
God. Never leaves. Unwavering

For the mother who worked in emergency services

memories lose their colour
and complexion over time
but it doesn't make it easier
now that she is a mother

  : child removed from wreckage
    vitals unknown

other mothers, bless their hearts,
just call it anxiety
and offer simple solutions
as does the preacher
but seldom ask where it is from

  : two children
    punctures to torso

and even if they did ask
to speak of it, spreads it
though she sees a therapist
for this complex soul-soup

  : female / pregnant
  suspected overdose

made from PTSD,
moral injury
vicarious trauma,
and a great deal of hope
that she will be able
to hold her own children
in everyday places,
along with her faith
and friends
and memories that come
from serving the suffering.

On Trauma

I am incredibly grateful for the way scientific research is now validating and exposing the devastating effects of trauma on the human body, soul and spirit. For too long we have been pointing the finger and trying to mend the symptoms and coping mechanisms of unresolved trauma, with no sustainable results. For example, simply treating addictions with medication, without addressing the underlying trauma, has been found to be far less effective long term. Also, we are beginning to see that trauma has many faces. Years ago, I came across work by people like Dr. Jim Wilder and the team at The LifeModel. I discovered trauma not only comes when bad things happen to us or we are exposed to trauma vicariously (as in the last poem), but trauma is experienced when we don't get the things we were created for (e.g., love, safe affection, safe environment, pleasure, nurture, blessing, etc.). I explain it this way: If you imagine a plant in a yard that needs to be destroyed, you can either take an axe and cut it down, or you can cover it with a blanket and starve it of sunlight and water. Both the act against it and the neglect of it are traumatic.

The following poems include a strong theme of trauma, beginning with a poem I wrote with a couple of loving friends in mind. They found themselves at life's edge, wondering if handing their entire life back to God would be the fastest way to freedom from the complex pressures church pastors face today. You will also see a piece I wrote for those who grew up in dysfunctional homes, particularly those who are now Adult Children of Alcoholics (ACOA). In my opinion, ACOA is a term too many people are unfamiliar with but deserve to know because most are living with trauma from carers with addictions.

The QR code at the beginning of the book points to some resources that may help.

For the pastor who nearly died by suicide

And the sheep had no idea
their shepherd had leant over life's edge
and was staring into the relief
death was offering.

When hope and strength leave you
and the weight of a flock
rests upon your shoulders
you are forgiven
for considering
an 'out' like this.

"Why does he not just trust God?"
the sheep murmured.
Which was ironic,
seeing they expected
so much from their shepherd.

"If he is gone, how will we be fed and led?"
they continued.
Which was ironic,
seeing they confessed
the Lord was their shepherd.

And on that ledge
out of earshot from the sheep
the shepherd heard the voice
he'd been longing
to be strengthened by.
"Don't jump.
   Just fall
      into me
         and a new way
            of being."

Needless to say,
the sheep were shocked
when things changed.
But they grew anyway.
Finding green pastures on their own.

And the shepherd learned
to breathe again
to enjoy the meadow
and walk lockstep
with his friend and lover
the Shepherd King.

To the one who, as a child, watched their father die slowly

You did all
a child can do
in such a position.

You wanted to play the healer
but were resigned to the role
of witness

to the slowest ascent
towards heaven's gate
watching

the one you call 'Dad'
be robbed
of life and years.

So much faded slowly.
Dreams and hopes.
Views of God too.

Life showed you its hand -
terribly fragile.

I've always wondered
why superheroes
lose their dads in childhood
but it's no mystery to you

you watched the one
who was supposed to be strong
lose a long and painful battle

and you knew
it would take
grit beyond tears

to carry this memory
beneath your Bruce Wayne facade
and avenge his death

by choosing life
every
fragile
day.

'Dear ACOA'
For the one with the alcoholic parent

It's a four-letter word
and it's not kind
or love, or hope.
The word that best describes
growing up with
an alcoholic parent
is shit.

And it lingers for years.
Stalking you into adulthood.
Smearing itself on the edge
of broken promises
making reality hard to grasp.
Silencing speech.
Scapegoating smellers.
It's shit.

The unspoken rules.
The sense you get
that you're second
to a substance
because they'd rather booze-up
than buy you shoes
or a basic meal.

By the way, 'best go to bed,
they're still at the bottle shop.
It's shit.

And all the ways you blame yourself -
performing through perfection
for attention
then swinging to rebellion,
anything
anything to be seen
and loved
and held
more than a bottle
for the beloved you are
and your heart is bleeding.
It's shit.

And I'm sorry.
And I'd love to tell you
it doesn't matter
 but it does
 because you do
 and always have.
And that deep anger
and sadness that seeps
from your scars are normal,

and they exist
because you know
deep in your love-seeded soul
that you did nothing
to deserve the neglect,
or the harm or the shame
from that parent
who may have loved you
but failed terribly
at loving themselves
or parenting themselves
with any maturity.
It's shit.

And I'm sorry.
And I'm praying
that you keep walking
towards the light
of healing
and wholeness
as slowly as you need
with guides
and friends
at your side.

For the one recovering from fatigue

Life moved faster than she could run
and before long, her best intentions
and desire to keep up were not enough.
Adrenaline and anxiety are perfect
for flighted escapes and armoured fights
but move like rockets, not gliders. Before long,
all her tanks were empty, and elevation was low.
She didn't really crash, she just barely
left the ground. God knows she tried.
                    God knows she cried out.
                    God knew she needed rest.
And just like that she discovered
she was strong enough to trust
and lean on others, to ask for help
and let the earth spin on its own axis.
And she is still learning to take each hour
as it greets her. And she is still learning to say no.
To disappoint the desperate.
And find God in the ground and wildflowers.

'Palettes Beyond Pain'
For the artist on the healing journey

A palette of watercolour
steeped in trauma and left to run,
That's how I painted my life.

It's not exactly what God gave me
but what my childhood shaped,
and I did my very best.

It's complex, this PTSD.
For so long
I took these dark colours as normal.

Borrowing, instead, from others -
painting bright futures for them.
All the while, my own palette lay drying up.
Each well terribly similar.

It's complex, this PTSD.
All that is in me now
wants to paint life as a masterpiece.
And all that is in me now
wearies, painting pleasing facades.
So with the strength I have left,
(most times, with help)
I'm fighting to find my own colours -
scraping back the painful shades
revealing what I can only describe
as spectacular and beloved.

On Religious Shame

Over the past few decades, authors and researchers like Dr. Brené Brown and others have done an outstanding job explaining what shame is, how it is different from guilt, how it comes to us and how it may be healed. What is rarely addressed or researched are the effects of religious shame; that is, the shame developed and experienced in connection to one's religion.

Christianity is my context, and I must say, we have a history terribly rich with shame. Without diverging too much, it is worth noting that shame has played an interesting role in Western society because of the way Christians have employed it over the centuries as a means of social control, or an unwanted feeling that needs to be assuaged.

In the early church, particularly during times of heavy persecution, shame was to be embraced and transformed into something glorious, that in a way, shamed the shamers. Imagine it's 100AD, and a group of Jesus followers, naked, in the middle of a Roman coliseum are about to be attacked by lions with thousands of people watching, cheering and jeering. Silence enters the arena as they smile, turn to the leader's high booth and begin to sing songs of worship to God. As martyrs, they embrace the shame and transform it into a moment of glory. Shame, in turn, falls back upon all those who dare to participate and support such an event. These kinds of events took shame on an interesting journey over the centuries and across seas and cultures. Along the way, it was split and divided into guilt and shame. Each played a unique role, and was explained in clever cognitive terms, but hard to distinguish when felt. Each was either embraced as a social catalyst for right-doing and/or despised as a feeling to be avoided.

What I find both fascinating and disturbing, is the way shame still masks itself in an invisible religious cloak. It has infiltrated the way so many

Christians automatically think and act, myself included. I am doing my best to increase my awareness of it, but I keep bumping into it, especially when it is informed by a non-compassionate theology in myself or others. In our fight against shame, some have suggested that honour go before it as the antidote. Others suggest it be embraced in martyrdom so that glory follows it. Whatever the case, I think the global Body of Christ has a long way to go when it comes to dismantling and decolonizing thinking and behaviour around topics of gender, race, sexuality, capitalism, ableism, mental-health, suicide, trauma, church leadership, marriage and so much more.

Although a number of the previous poems, such as the one on abortion, touch on areas of religious shame, I think the following poems highlight its hideous face in a greater way. The first poem addresses the way religious shame affects those living with illness that may have them arriving to church aided, in this case, in a wheelchair. Religious shame has a way of adding insult to injury, especially working through people who can't see past their own discomfort or opportunity to turn the person into a project. I have found co-dependency and religious showmanship are rife in some denominations, particularly Pentecostal and Charismatic churches. The second poem addresses sexuality and same-sex attraction. A topic that has been, and will continue to be, debated among Christians for some time, unfortunately. Again, religious shame plays its terrible hand as a dignity thief, along with a skewed theology and terribly poor dialogue around sex and sexuality in the church.

In the violent wake of the same-sex attraction debate lay thousands of lives strewn and despised. We often forget that the wounded are not only those trying to hold within themselves two group identities which have a history of hating one another, gay & Christian. But also, those who love, support, parent and friend them lay wounded and confused by religious shame.

Personally, I have a strong sense that Jesus refuses to march with oppressive armies that use an alchemy of religious shame as a weapon. Instead, He can be found as the co-suffering Christ and healer of hearts in the field of the wounded, oppressed and misunderstood - holding them close to His chest, whispering their names as a poem of peace.

For the one who comes to church in a wheelchair

I cannot stand
or stand the pity and platitudes,
words laden with guilt -
for years now
I have been wheeled into the building
to be part of the Sunday gathering:
  daughter on lap
  husband holding handles
but it's like you are more troubled
with God not healing me, than I am.
In fact, we didn't come at great expense
to beg or be made into
a sermon illustration
or your next healing project.
I do not need more faith or pity.
I came here to worship.
To love and be loved.
And I know Jesus made the lame to walk.
Don't you think I've asked?
He also rebuked the religious shamers,
but I'm failing to see the change in you
(to be honest).

Don't you know, when the music plays
and my frail fingers
hold the broken body bread
my spirit soars
and my adoration transcends
the bounds of what you call
bent or broken
and I dance in perichoresis
with Jesus behind me
gladly pushing me around
not troubled by my state
but simply seeing me
and loving me
as I am
not as I should be -
which is all I ask of you.
Which is what I pray for you.

For the one whose confession set her free

she went from youth leader to leper
in a single confession.
no audience of reason
so swift was the response.
of course, this wouldn't happen at every church,
just most.

at this youth group
girls had to be attracted to boys,
or vice versa. never the same or both.

and the leaders didn't understand
the prayer that went into that meeting.
some by words. some silence.
mostly tears, fear and trembling
something in her braved to believe
that she WAS made in God's image.
she WAS fearfully and wonderfully made.
at least, this is what she heard on Sundays.

stripped of title and stood down,
what is a young woman to do?
she didn't sleep with anyone
   unlike others she knew.
   all of whom were forgiven
   and simply told to sin no more.
but this?

it is no surprise
she found comfort in Trinity
just as she had always done.
and found a faith community
that doesn't tolerate her -
it welcomes her.
and when the pastor preaches unconditional love
and Christ's message of acceptance
her lips and heart say amen.

For the one who was taken advantage of

And he told her
That according to the text
Her body was a temple
But he failed
To hand her the key
Which she took as normal
And he left it messy
And now she's charged for therapy
When he should be charged in court.
God, have mercy

Poem for the brave

It's the way you held your mouth
  when the news reached the edge of your ears
Dry lips pressed together
  in efforts to stop more life escaping
Deep sharp breaths through rapidly closing nostrils
  followed by eyes damning rivers

Oh my
 you were a brave soul

All of heaven knows you were
  and ranks you with the saints

Now, please don't think for a moment
  that being brave looks like silence
  like holding it all forever
  like protecting transgressors
  like taking lies to the grave

Maybe now, bravery looks different
  like finding your own voice
  like giving over to tears
  like telling your story
  like really, really loving your self

On Marriage

Religious shame, trauma and loss continue to play in the orchestra of marriage. I don't know of a single person who went to the wedding altar and said 'I do' with the intention of it not working out (Sure, they may have had doubts.).

Nor do I know many people who enjoyed the separation and divorce process, particularly in Church where the (ridiculous) expectation is that you move through life free of pain, suffering and complexity. The next few poems speak of divorce, betrayal and unwanted singleness. This theme was common in many who shared their stories with me. If you can relate, I do hope you feel seen and held in these pieces.

For the woman waiting for a man to marry

To the one waiting
dreaming
praying
and believing
for that soul mate
to arrive
and see the world
through their eyes
but are so tired -
losing or lost hope,
I'm sorry.

I'm sorry for the times
others have told you
to just keep praying
like you can twist God's arm
to make a man appear
when all around you
others who prayed,
asked and waited
have remained single
and now you wonder
how to pray,
if at all.

And I'm sorry for the times
people have shamed you
for your longing
for your past,
for a close friend,
someone to love
and be loved by,
like the longing is
forbidden
and the desire for sex
is carnal or wrong.
When it's not wrong
and neither are you.
You are human
like Jesus
who embodies intimacy
in the Trinity -
so how can this
be a crime?

And if I had the power
to grant permission
with a poem
for these desires
to be eliminated,

I would not.
Instead, I would
grant you permission
to long and yearn
for union and friendship
with all that you are
without shame or reserve
without guarantee of outcome
except that you'll feel
more alive
more pain
more of you
and possibly more loved
than those who take
their man for granted
which you will never do.

For the divorced ones

You said I do
and you didn't
intend for it to end
the way that it did.
God knows.

And God knows
how much it takes
to hold
beautiful and broken
people together.
More than you know

And more than you know
stood at the altar
with hope and dreams
of building a life together
which you did.
For a time.

And for a time
it worked
in its own way
till things
got in the way
so you parted ways.
This is your story.

And this is your story
but not the final chapter
so unfold those fingers
pick up hope's healing pen
and write with what you have -
  the breath in your lungs
    the faithful morning sun
      the Divine at your side
        and lessons from the night.

For the one who was betrayed.

(To the betrayer)

There is a tree by our home
that fell in a storm
on the path
I walked to belonging.

I assumed this was our path,
and perhaps it was,
but the storm -
that was your betrayal.

Torn from the earth.
Branches broken.
Leaves strewn like confetti
on our wedding day.

Roots, now exposed,
shamefully waving at passers-by,
remind me
of what was sown in secret.

Trunk, now splintered,
piercing those who dare to pry,
remind me
of your unrepentant reasoning.

I've been tempted,
more than once,
to nest in the wreckage
but you won't find me there.

Instead, I'll be in the forest
forging new paths
through forgiveness
and a fog of grief,
vowing to love myself
more than you ever did.

On Everything Else

I wanted to end the book with some pieces that I felt were too important to leave out simply because they didn't fit the other themes. I created the next poems for those who wrote in, plus a few personal ones that are similar in tone to those in *The Wrestle*; that is, honest poems of my spiritual journey.

'How to Settle Down'
For the wandering migrant

Imagine yourself as a tree
moving from garden to garden
transplanted by weather or will.

No need to pretend
that displacement is easy -
plants have withered before you.

But know that life welcomes you
and dares you
to dream just enough

that you belong here now.
So whether you wish to stay
or scuttle through

allow yourself
to settle into the soil
knowing the earth is no man's

but the roots
are
yours.

How to have hot conversations on conspiracy topics with those you love

Before you start, decide what you'd like.
If being right matters less than love,
this can help, but also make things harder.

Be sure to stand your ground
wherever that may be. Imagine a broad field,
not a ladder or stairs. Nothing with heights.

If you like, consider chitchat as foreplay.
Call it that, just for laughs
You will need some joy in the room.

After you are all excited, or one of you is
(which, if you are both there in love
should please the other too),

applaud their efforts but tell them
it is your turn. Keep in mind the intention
you began with, and risk the honest question

of whether you both think you have made
anything good together. If there is no new life,
make the decision and make it clear

you can't keep meeting like this.
If need be, tell them you feel uncomfortable.
If they refuse to stop, step away and make it known

you are simply not enjoying their company.
Never forget, all this will pass.
What will be, will be - and they may be right.

Enough Words

I will not pray or prophesy a promised outcome
as if to twist God's arm into submission

no

this moment is too precious for petition
too sacred for solutions

too holy for anything other
than being
seen in loving silence

The saving I need

I used to cry out to you
For you
With fervour and volume
Not ceasing to bid
For divine intervention
Asking you to come
Like a rider of clouds
Like Deus Ex Machina
Like a warrior king

I'd petition you
To deliver me
And save me
From my suffering
From my lack
From my angst
And you did
You did
Till you didn't

It's like you stopped
Stopped allowing
Me to see you that way
Far away
Worlds away
Pushed away
So you delivered me
You saved me

You saved me from the lie
That you were distant
That you could leave me
Forsake me
Go against your word
Your nature
And be anywhere other
Than with me
Be anyone other
Than Immanuel

So, I quit working
Quit striving
Allowing myself to rest
I took a break
From burnt offerings
Burning myself
Beating myself
And started loving myself
Like you do
I started learning
What it meant to be me
With you by my side
And it was great
Really great
Till it wasn't
And I needed saving again

You see
To know you are with me
Is a truth
And a joy
But a by-my-side
Best-friend-saviour
Way of knowing you
Still has me separate
Separate from union
Separate from oneness
Separate from discovering
My place in the divine dance
Which is where
You brought me
Eternally
Which is crazy
Which changes everything
But I'm learning
Slowly learning
That the truth of my being
  My very being
Is you
You

About Now

And it's about now
I wonder why
I made the choices I did
when regret descends
to the pit of my stomach
with a heaviness
only tears
and deep sighs
can translate
into prayer

And it's about now
I look to distraction
for ways
to stop the loss
from dropping lower
into my legs
rendering me
limp and lame
and unable
to walk
on my own

And it's about now
I turn to God
with scant words
hoping They know
how I feel
hoping for relief
from the shame
without revealing
the reason
it arrived

And it's about now
I reach out
for the inviting hands
of an invisible God
and trek
towards regret
knowing over time
ashes and mourning
become beauty and joy

in Their presence
in Their faces
in confession
in forgiveness
in Their truth
in Their child
in me
about now

As a kind of bookend to this special collection, I'd like to leave you with a blessing. I wrote this piece when I had finished writing poems for all those who wrote in. Thank you for taking the time to journey with me and those whose lives are represented here. I pray you felt surrounded.

A blessing of surrounding

May you be surrounded
by those who surround you
with hugs that hold your world together
words that ground your feet to belong
joy that strengthens your heart to endure
and eyes that hope to see yours again

So I Wrote You A Poem
available in eBook and Audiobook format.

Also by David Tensen:

The Wrestle
Poems of divine disappointment and discovery
2020

w: www.davidtensen.com
e: david@davidtensen.com

ig: @david_tensen
fb: /davidtensenwriter
tw: @davidtensen

SCAN WITH SMARTPHONE FOR URL
AND RELATED RESOURCES

About the Author

Australian poet David Tensen brings form and beauty to our deep spiritual yearnings. Drawing from decades of experience in pastoral care, leadership and spiritual development, his poems have found their way into hearts of many. Raw, honest, accessible and prophetic, David's writings uncover pain and bring healing to it.

David, his wife Natalie, and three children live in Queensland, Australia.

Interesting Fact:

A majority of the poems in this book were typed on manual typewriters from David's collection. The most used typewriter was a 1960s Olivetti Lettera 32